SPOTTED STRIPED FISH

and

FISH

Written By
Jenny Dearinger and Carrie Johnson Parker-Warren

Illustrated By
Jenny Dearinger

Photograph of ocean coral by Jenny Dearinger

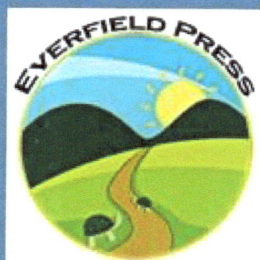

EVERFIELD PRESS

In Dedication

I would like to
dedicate this book to
ALL
Boys and Girls who make
Healthy Choices
To solve problems and
disagreements in
*Peaceful, Kind,
Respectful, Thoughtful*
and
Lawful ways.

-Ms. Parker-Warren

In Recognition

I would like to recognize
the
RIGHT
of EVERY
boy and girl
to wear a hoodie
or
sleep in their own bed
without fear.
-Ms. Dearinger

*"A person's a person,
no matter
how small"*

-Dr. Seuss

Spotted Fish lived in a towering, flowering coral of bright reds, greens, and blues.

Spotted Fish's mom and dad gave him all the toys and food he wanted.

His parents told him he was special because he lived in a big coral house and his scales were spotted.

Striped Fish lived in a dark and chilly cave.

The only toy he had was a crab doll. Sometimes he did not get enough fish food.

His parents told him that he was special because of the good he could do for others.

They taught him that the size of a fish's home or the pattern on his scales was not as important as sharing, helping, and caring.

1st DAY of SCHOOL

Spotted Fish and Striped Fish met on the first day of school.

At snack time, the teacher, Mrs. Catfish, handed each little fish three crackers. Spotted Fish gobbled up his crackers.

He wanted more, so he took one of Striped Fish's crackers.

Mrs. Catfish said, "Spotted Fish, you may not take crackers from Striped Fish. How would you feel if Striped Fish took your cracker?"

Confused, Spotted Fish said, "But, I thought I was special and could have whatever I wanted. I want Striped Fish's cracker."

Striped Fish's mom and dad had taught him to share with others.

Striped Fish said with compassion, "Fish are fish no matter the pattern on their scales. I'll share."

Striped Fish gave Spotted Fish one of his crackers.

The next day,
each fish built a
sandcastle
at recess.

**Spotted Fish's sandcastle
was drippy and sloppy.**

Striped Fish built a tall castle with turrets and ramparts. He even decorated it with seashells.

Spotted Fish *kicked* over Striped Fish's beautiful castle.

Mrs. Catfish said, "Spotted Fish, you may not kick over Striped Fish's castle. How would you feel if Striped Fish kicked over your castle?"

Spotted Fish said in a confused voice, "But I thought since I live in a towering, flowering coral, Striped Fish couldn't have a better sandcastle than me."

Striped Fish's mom and dad had taught him to help others.

Striped Fish said with patience, "Fish are fish no matter the pattern on their scales. I'll help you build a tall castle."

In math class, Spotted Fish could not figure out a problem, so he cried.

2+2+2=?

In PE, he buried the ball so no one could play.

At recess, he pulled dorsal fins and kicked sand.

Mrs. Catfish sat Spotted Fish in the corner.

Striped Fish swam up and put his fin around Spotted Fish.

Striped Fish's mom and dad had taught him to care for others.

He said gently, "Fish are fish no matter the pattern on their scales. Sometimes we all need a hug."

It was the fourth day of school. Striped Fish was late. Striped Fish missed the bus, which meant he also missed breakfast.

SCHOOL BUS

At snack time, Spotted
Fish shared
his cracker with
Striped Fish.

Striped Fish got behind in math because he had missed the directions.

Spotted Fish helped Striped Fish figure out the math problem.

Striped Fish was so tired, he took a nap at recess instead of playing.

When Striped Fish woke up,
Spotted Fish said,
"I built a tall sandcastle just
for you."

Spotted Fish's sharing, helping, and caring brought tears to Striped Fish's eyes.

"I don't know what to say, Spotted Fish," said Striped Fish.

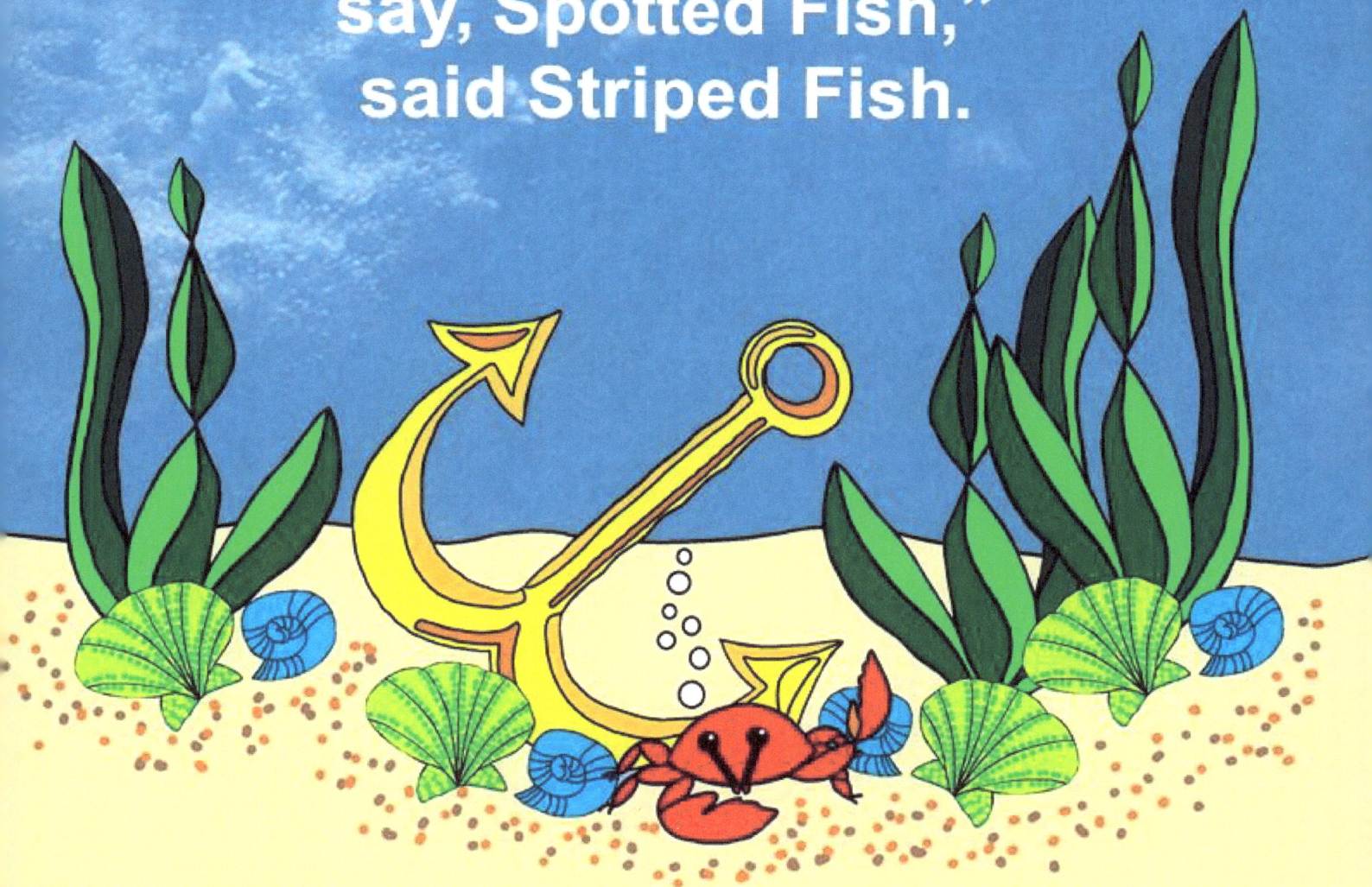

Spotted Fish's friend had taught him how to be a real friend.

Spotted Fish put his fin around Striped Fish and said with an understanding smile,

"Fish are fish no matter the pattern on their scales. We take care of each other."

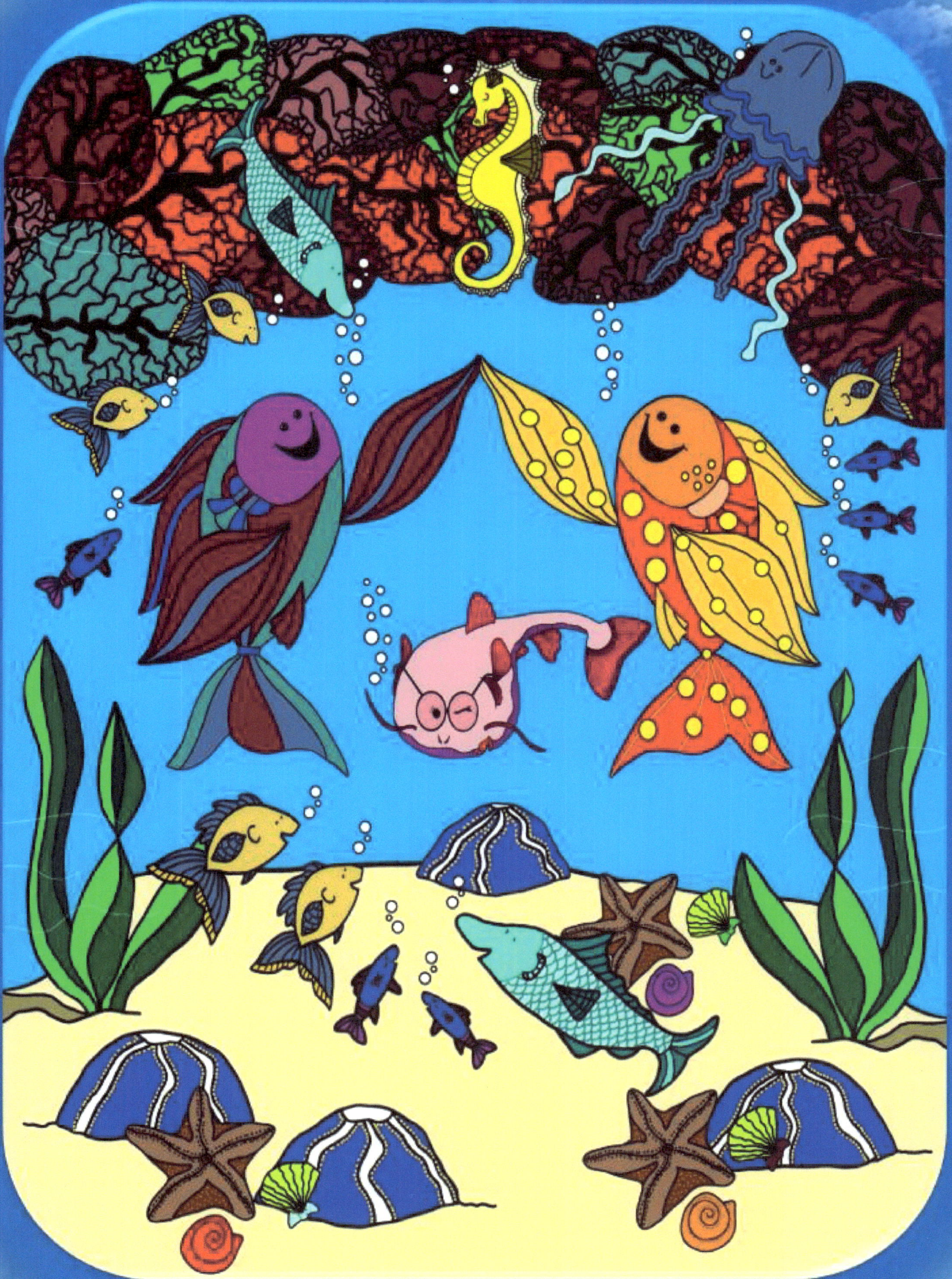

Parents and Educators Guide

This story presents two issues: **Social Equality and Racial Equality**. You can teach your child(ren) to treat all people with the same compassion and empathy.

Major Points-

- **Empathy** is putting yourself in the other person's position and understanding their feelings.

- Teaching your child empathy gives your child the tools to solve everyday conflicts with others and to combat racism and social injustice.

- **Social Equality** is when people of all types are treated with the same regard to civil rights and justice; kindness and fairness. Unequal physical conditions (such as housing or economics) do not make one fish more privileged than another.

  Spotted Fish learned lessons of Social Equality. Spotted Fish learned that just because one person is born into a comfortable state of being does not mean that they are "better than" people born into less desirable conditions. This can also be applied to other human traits such as sexuality, ability (or disability), religion, or heritage.

- **Racial Equality** is treating people with the same respect, tolerance, and justice regardless of skin color. Racism is a method used by some people to identify a person's value by the color of their skin. Skin color is determined by the amount of melanin in your skin. Skin color has nothing to do with behavior: if you are a good person or not.

  Spotted Fish learned lessons of Racial Equality. Spotted Fish learned that "Fish are fish, no matter the pattern on their scales." Children can learn that people are people no matter how much melanin is in their skin and all people are entitled to the same respect.

- **<u>Reciprocity</u>** is expecting the same response that you give. Social Equality *AND* Racial Equality can be taught by modeling 'reciprocity.'

  In Spotted Fish's case, he learned, if you do not want someone to take your crackers, don't take theirs. If you do not want someone to knock down your sandcastle, don't knock down theirs. If you want to be treated with compassion and kindness, you need to treat others the same way.

- **Start teaching your children at a very young age to practice the lessons of reciprocity. Another way to say this is, follow the lessons of**

  THE GOLDEN RULE
  "Do Unto Others as You Would Have Them Do Unto You."

QUESTIONS About
Spotted Fish and Striped Fish

1. What makes Spotted Fish and Striped Fish the same?

2. What makes the two fish different?

3. What did Spotted Fish learn from Striped Fish?

4. Can friends be different on the outside and come from different homes, or do they have to be the same?

5. How important are sharing, helping, and caring?

6. If your friend took your cracker, what would you do?

7. If your friend kicked over your sandcastle, what would you do?

8. If your friend was having a bad day, what would you do?

9. Even if you are the nicest person in the world, you may not be able to teach others to be nice. Does that mean you should stop being nice?

10. How can you set a good example like Spotted Fish and Striped Fish?

11. BONUS QUESTION-
    What is the *REAL* treasure in this story?

EMPATHY WORKSHEET #1

"Identifying How I FEEL"

This worksheet is the first in a series that teach children empathy. Empathy leads to a greater understanding of Social and Racial Equality issues. To be a good friend (to show empathy), children must be able to demonstrate understanding of the emotions driving the other person. But first, children must give **names** to those emotions and understand themselves. Read each sentence to your child. Ask your child to fill in the blanks. No doubt you'll learn a lot about your child.

I feel **ANGRY,** when_____.
(Possible Answers- I don't win; someone gets more than me)

I can tell I'm **ANGRY** when I _____.
(Possible Answers- Bite; Break things; throw a temper tantrum)

I feel **GRUMPY** when_____.
 (Possible Answers- I don't get enough sleep; someone took my toy)

I can tell I'm **GRUMPY** when I _____.
(Possible answers- Withdraw into myself; throw a temper tantrum)

I feel **SAD** when _____.
(Possible Answers- Someone leaves me; someone yells at me)

I can tell I'm **SAD** when I _____.
(Possible Answers- Cry; scratch; bite; throw a temper tantrum)

I feel **EMBARRASSED** when _____.
(Possible Answer- Laughs at me)

I can tell I'm **EMBARRASSED** when I _____.
(Possible Answers- Throw a temper tantrum; break things)

I feel **SCARED** when _____.
(Possible Answers- I might get hurt; I'm startled)

I can tell I'm **SCARED** when I _____.
(Possible Answers- Cry; run away; become clingy)

EMPATHY WORKSHEET #2

"Identifying What I NEED"

This worksheet is the second in a series of worksheets building understanding of Social and Racial Equality in your child. Once children can identify their own feelings, they need to know what they need in order to correct that feeling. Then they can **transfer** how they feel to how others feel under similar conditions. Ask your child these questions and fill in the blanks. Read each sentence to your child. Ask your child to fill in the blanks. No doubt you'll learn a lot about your child.

To help me calm down when I am **ANGRY** I need _____.
(Possible Answers- something to make me happy; food; a hug; to be left alone)

To help me get over feeling **GRUMPY** I need _____.
(Possible Answers- food; sleep; to be left alone; something to make me happy)

To help me get over feeling **SAD** I need _____.
(Possible Answers- food; a hug; a kind word; sleep)

To help me stop feeling **EMBARRASSED** I need _____.
(Possible Answer- Not to be laughed at; a kind word; to go on to another activity, to go somewhere alone)

To help me stop feeling **SCARED** I need _____.
(Possible Answers- to feel safe, a hug, the bad thing to go away)

EMPATHY WORKSHEET #3

"Identifying How my Friend FEELS"

This worksheet is the third in a series that teach children empathy. Empathy leads to a greater understanding of Social and Racial Equality standards. Your child is beginning to identify behaviors in others that they themselves feel. Read each sentence to your child. Ask your child to fill in the blanks. No doubt you'll learn a lot about your child.

Something happened and my friend looks **ANGRY.**

I can tell my friend feels **ANGRY** because_____.
(Possible Answers- Bite; Break things; throw a temper tantrum)

Something happened and my friend looks **GRUMPY.**

I can tell my friend feels **GRUMPY** because_____.
(Possible answers- they withdraw; throw a temper tantrum; throw things)

Something happened and my friend looks **SAD.**

I can tell my friend feels **SAD** when they _____.
(Possible Answers- Cry; scratch; bite; throw a temper tantrum)

Something happened and my friend looks **EMBARRASSED.**

I can tell my friend feels **EMBARRASSED** because _____.
(Possible Answers- Get red in the face; turn away; cry; throw a temper tantrum; break things)

Something happened and my friend looks **SCARED.**

I can tell my friend feels **SCARED** because _____.
(Possible Answers- Cry; run away; become clingy)

Empathy Worksheet #4

"Identifying What My Friend NEEDS"

This is the fourth worksheet in a series on Building Understanding of Social and Racial Equality. Teach your child **Reciprocity.** Reciprocity is giving to others what they would like to receive in the same type of circumstance. Read each sentence to your child. Ask your child to fill in the blanks. No doubt you'll learn a lot about how well you are modeling social and racial equality behaviors for your child to emulate.

When my friend is feeling **ANGRY**, I can give my friend the same thing I would want, like _____.
(Possible Answers- I can listen without interrupting; repeat what they say so they know I understand; give them space)

When my friend is feeling **GRUMPY**, I can give my friend the same thing I would want, like _____.
(Possible Answers- I can give my friend space; be quiet; listen, something to eat)

When my friend is feeling **SAD**, I can give my friend the same thing I would want, like _____.
(Possible Answers- I can listen; give a hug; offer to help; say 'I'm sorry.')

When my friend is feeling **EMBARRASSED**, I can give my friend the same thing I would want, like _____.
(Possible Answers- Listen; share a story; give a hug)

When my friend is feeling **SCARED**, I can give my friend the same thing I would want, like _____.
(Possible Answers- I can listen; be understanding; tell a grownup)

About the Authors

Carrie Johnson Parker-Warren is the author of several memoires: *Carrie's Memories, Things My Mama Used to Say,* and *The Johnson-Morgan Family Memories.* Her latest endeavor is *Matriarchs and Matrons: Honoring Mothers and Daughters.* Ms. Parker has strong roots in North Central Florida. She was born and raised in Ocala and has spent most of her adult life in Gainesville. Ms. Parker is a prominent member and leading female figure the Gainesville community and has multiple degrees from Florida Agricultural and Mechanical University (FAMU), the University of South Florida, and the University of Florida. Ms. Parker spent a career in education as a Secondary School Administrator. She has one son, Scott, who lives in Los Angeles, CA. When Carrie is not busy writing or volunteering in one of many community organizations, she loves to play tennis, read, decorate, and hunt for antiques (junktiquing).

Jenny Dearinger is the author/illustrator of several children's books: *A Stone's Crow, Fireball Tennis,* and *Journey to Moose's* to name a few. She received her bachelor's degree in Elementary Education from Florida State University. She taught within several school systems in the State of Florida including Escambia and Alachua Counties. Currently, Ms. Dearinger is a member and active participant in her two writing groups, Writer's Alliance of Gainesville, and the national organization, Society of Children's Book Writers and Illustrators (SCBWI). When not writing and illustrating children's books, Ms. Dearinger enjoys her hobbies as a lapidarist (rock cutter), jewelry designer, and tennis player.

www.ingramcontent.com/pod-product-compliance
Lightning Source LLC
Chambersburg PA
CBHW041544260326

41914CB00015B/1546